THE MINI ADVENTURES OF
DANNY AND THE DEPLOYER

Advantage BOOKS

JUANDA RUTH BRYANT

Illustrations by David Brian Craig

First Printing: May 2017
17 18 19 20 21 22 23 24   10 9 8 7 6 5 4 3 2 1
Printed in the United States of America

To the one who turned the Paige in my life.

"Hey mom! I had fun at school today!"
said Danny as he put on his seat belt.

"What did you learn today?" asked Mom.

"I can skip count!" Danny starts to count "2, 4, 6, 8, 10, 12..."

"That's so good Danny. I'm so proud of you," said Mom.

"Danny," Dad said, "I need to tell you something important. I am about to deploy."

"Dad, what does deploy mean?" asked Danny.

Dad explained, "deploy means to move troops into position for military action. My job is to protect and serve the country and sometimes that means to travel far away.

All the training I do in the military prepares me for the mission."

Dad saw that Danny was sad so he reached for the surprise...it is a "Deployer!"

The Deployer is a toy Soldier that transforms.

Danny thought, this was so cool that he jumped up and hugged Dad.

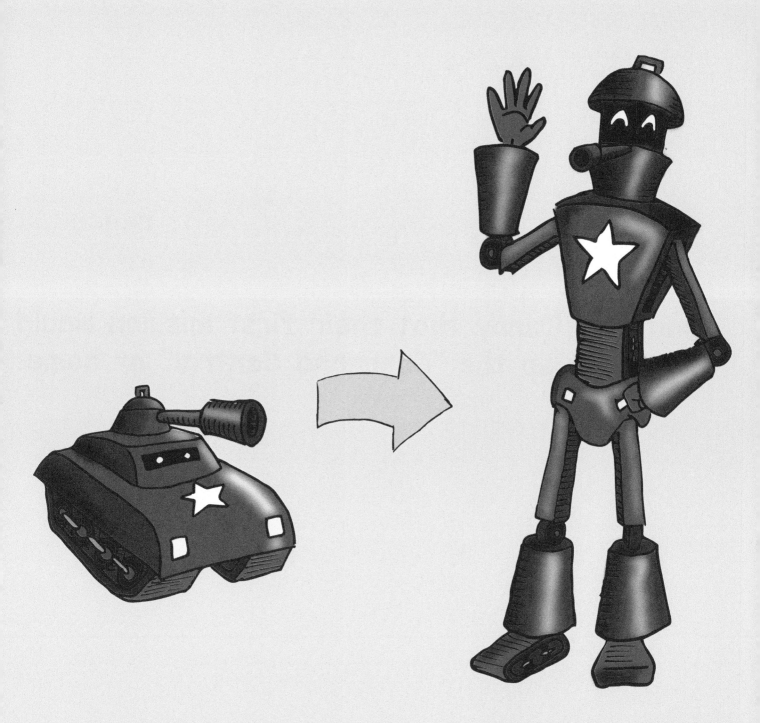

Dad told Danny that their first mission would be to set up the "Command Central" at home.

In "Command Central," we hung up clocks to tell my time and daddy's time. We made a place called "mail for daddy." Then we put up a poster of the world and a calendar.

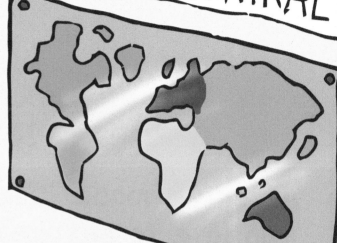

After we made "Command Central," we stayed up late to eat popcorn and watch a movie.

ABOUT THE AUTHOR

Juanda R. Bryant is a certified educator with a Bachelor's of Science in Psychology. Her outstanding dedication to her school and students has made her the recipient of the "Outstanding Educator Award." Juanda is a decorated military veteran who served 12 years in the United States Army as a Transportation Coordinator. Juanda has a combat tour to Iraq and Afghanistan.

As part of her role in the military, she operated as a Family Readiness Group Liaison preparing Soldiers and families for deployment. In this position, she discovered there was a need for engaging and educating children as it pertained to deployment of family members. This is where this exciting book had its genesis.

The Mini-Adventures of Danny and the Deployer is a book that will provide children an identifiable character that can relate to growing up in a military family. Moreover, it is a book designed to captivate the Emergent Reader.

Juanda comes from a linage of family members who have served this great nation. Her father, brothers, uncles, aunts, and cousins have all dedicated their lives to the United States Military.

In addition to teaching, supporting the local Army Reserve Unit, and participating in multiple community service groups; Juanda loves spending time with family and friends by playing Taboo or singing karaoke.

For more information contact:

Juanda Ruth Bryant
C/O Advantage Books
P.O. Box 160847
Altamonte Springs, FL 32716

info@advbooks.com

To purchase additional copies of this book visit our bookstore website at: www.advbookstore.com

Longwood, Florida, USA
"we bring dreams to life"™
www.advbookstore.com

CPSIA information can be obtained
at www.ICGtesting.com
Printed in the USA
BVOW05s1424040517

483156BV00005B/10/P